THE
WORLD SERIES

by
Jane Duden

CRESTWOOD HOUSE
New York

Maxwell Macmillan Canada
Toronto

Maxwell Macmillan International
New York Oxford Singapore Sydney

Library of Congress Cataloging-in-Publication Data
Duden, Jane
  The World Series / by Jane Duden.
    p. cm. — (Sportslines)
  Summary: Surveys the notable events in the history of the annual baseball playoffs
between the National and American Leagues.
    ISBN 0-89686-724-2
    1. World Series (Baseball)—History—Juvenile literature. [1. World Series (Baseball)—
History. 2. Baseball—History.] I. Title. II. Series.
GV878.4.D83   1992
796.357'646—dc20   91-23790

Photo Credits
Cover: AP—Wide World Photos
Northeastern University: 4
ACME: 7, 17
National Baseball Hall of Fame: 8, 11, 12, 18, 20, 22, 25, 27, 34, 36, 39, 40, 42, 44, 45
UPI: 14
AP—Wide World Photos: 29, 33
Dick Raphael: 31
National Baseball League: 37

Copyright © 1992 by Crestwood House, Macmillan Publishing Company

CRESTWOOD HOUSE

Macmillan Publishing Company   Maxwell Macmillan Canada, Inc.
866 Third Avenue   1200 Eglinton Avenue East
New York, NY 10022   Suite 200
                                   Don Mills, Ontario M3C 3N1

Macmillan Publishing Company is part of the Maxwell Communication Group of Companies.

Produced by Flying Fish Studio

Printed in the United States of America

First edition

10 9 8 7 6 5 4 3 2 1

Contents

The first World Series in 1903

Introduction

Every fall the World Series casts a spell over baseball fans everywhere. Even those who ignore baseball the rest of the year pay attention when the world championship starts! It's the super event when great teams clash. Underdogs upset favorites. Now you can be part of baseball history! Join baseball's greats for fantastic fielding. Thrilling baserunning. Dynamite hitting. Awesome pitching. Rarities, bloopers, and blunders. Turn the page for magic moments, highlights and lowlights of the Fall Classic—baseball's World Series!

Play Ball!

The first World Series was played in 1903. Baseball's National League had been around for 28 years. The American League (AL) was only three years old. The 1903 National League (NL) champs were the Pittsburgh Pirates. The American League champs were the Boston Pilgrims (the team that became the Red Sox). The series came about when the owner of the Pirates challenged Boston to a playoff series after the regular season had ended. He thought it would be a good way to put the upstart American League in its place. Boston took its place—ahead of the Pirates! With the pitching of Bill Dinneen and Cy Young, Boston won five of eight games to win the title.

Sitting One Out

The World Series was not played in 1904. The owner and manager of the lordly New York Giants (NL) refused to let his team play a team from "the minor league." The American League let it pass, but the fans didn't! They raised an uproar. The World Series was back in 1905. It has been held every October since then!

The Fall Classic

The World Series is called the Fall Classic. It ends months of hard work that started with spring training. The champions of the two major leagues meet in a showdown for the championship. The location of the opening game switches. One year it's in the American League city, in the National League's the next. After two games the series shifts to the other team's ballpark for games three, four and five. If more games are needed to determine a winner, the series goes back to the first park.

Ace Pitchers and Shutouts

The 1905 Series showed three future Hall of Fame pitchers at their best. Every one of the Series' five games was a shutout! (A shutout is a game in which the opposing team does not score.) Christy Mathewson and Joe McGinnity pitched for the New York Giants (NL). Chief Bender pitched for the Philadelphia Athletics (AL). Mathewson stood up to the pressure best and threw three scoreless games. The Giants won the championship, four games to one.

Christy Mathewson, in a pitching pose at the height of his career

Chicago, Chicago!

One of the biggest World Series upsets took place in 1906. The Chicago White Sox (AL) played the Chicago Cubs (NL). The Sox were hitting so poorly (a sorry .230) that they were called the "Hitless Wonders." The mighty Cubs had just won a record-setting 116 games during the season. (It's still the record.) George Rohe played in the series for the Sox only because another player was injured. He wasn't a very good player, and no one pinned hopes on him. But George became the star of the series. His triple—a three-base hit—in the first game led to a 2-1 victory. In game three, he hit another triple! It brought in all the runs for a 3-0 win. The underdog White Sox won the series, four games to two.

The White Sox beat the mighty Cubs in 1906, one of the biggest World Series upsets.

The 1912 Comedy of Errors

Never has baseball seen so many blunders and thrills as the 1912 World Series. It was hard to believe from teams like the New York Giants (NL) and the Boston Red Sox (AL). The Sox had a record of 105-47 while taking the pennant. It was a league record for wins that stood until 1931. They had Smokey Joe Wood, whose nickname came from his blazing fastball. Boston's outstanding outfield included Harry Hooper, Duffy Lewis and Tris Speaker. The New York Giants were just as impressive. They had the great Christy Mathewson, Rube Marquard and the league's earned run average (ERA) champ, Jeff Tesreau. But by the series' end, the ballplayers tallied up 31 official errors. There were blunders and confusion in every game!

Even the fans made a mistake. One day many of them left the ballpark believing that the losing team had really won. The score was Giants 2, Red Sox 1, with two outs. Darkness and fog were beginning to cover the stadium. Boston's batter hit Marquard's next pitch deep to center field. Giants center fielder Josh Devore raced after it. Deep in the fog near the fence, he finally caught the ball. It was the final out of the game. The game was over. Since the Giants' clubhouse was beyond the outfield fence, Devore saw no reason to come back to the infield. He went into the Giants' outfield clubhouse. Meanwhile the Red Sox fans saw their runners cross home plate. In the darkness and fog, they had not seen Devore's catch for the out. Thinking the Sox had won 3-2, they left the park celebrating. The next day they opened their newspapers to find that New York had won, 2-1!

By the end of the series, Boston had escaped with the championship, four games to three. But even they had to agree that if baseball was to survive as a serious game, it couldn't have another series like 1912's!

Yawner

The twelfth World Series, in 1915, was a low-scoring series. The Boston Red Sox (AL) beat the Philadelphia Phillies (NL) four games to one. The winning Red Sox made a total of only 12 runs in the five games!

Boston and the Babe

Game two of the 1916 series was a 14-inning thriller. Babe Ruth of the Boston Red Sox pitched the entire game. He gave up only six hits to the Brooklyn Dodgers. Boston and the Babe won the game 2-1. The championship was theirs, four games to one.

A Record For Ruth

The Boston Red Sox (AL) beat the Chicago Cubs (NL) four games to two in the 1918 World Series. The series is remembered for Babe Ruth's pitching. He hurled a number of scoreless innings—29 2/3. His record stood until 1961. Each player on the winning team received $1,102.51—the all-time low payment to World Series winners.

The Black Sox Scandal

In 1919 the Chicago White Sox were the best team in the American League. They won 88 games. Sox pitcher Ed Cicotte had a record of 29 wins, 7 losses. No one could touch him all year. Chicago was expected to beat the Cincinnati Reds (NL) in the series. But the underdog Cincinnati Reds knocked Cicotte all over the place. In game two, Chicago's most accurate pitcher, Claude Williams, walked six batters. The Sox lost 4-2. Stunned White Sox fans wondered what was going on. The White Sox won three games, but Cincinnati won the series.

The story came out in 1920. To the horror of all America, eight Chicago players had made a deal with the nation's leading gamblers. Gamblers had offered Cicotte and seven other White Sox players, including Williams and outfielder Shoeless Joe Jackson, a total of $100,000 to lose the series to the underdog Reds. The White Sox team was stained black. The eight "Black Sox" players were never found guilty in the courts. But they were banned from baseball for life. The White Sox floundered for decades. They would not finish higher than third until 1957.

The 1919 Chicago "Black" Sox

Babe Ruth

Babe Ruth Joins the Yankees

In 1920 the owner of the Boston Red Sox needed money. He sold "the Bambino," Babe Ruth, to the New York Yankees. It was a costly mistake. That year Babe Ruth hit 54 home runs for New York. Since then, the Sox have suffered what some call the Curse of the Bambino. The Yankees have won 22 World Series, the Sox none.

Giants Win

The New York Giants (NL) beat the Yankees (AL) in the 1921 series, five games to three. A bad arm kept Babe Ruth out of the last three games, and Giant pitching silenced Yankee bats. The Yankee team batting average was a puny .207.

Backstop Bungle

The 1924 series may be remembered for the most bungled play by a catcher. The catcher was the New York Giants' (NL) Hank Gowdy. It was the bottom of the twelfth inning. The score was 3-3. Muddy Ruel, a weak hitter, was at bat for the Washington Senators (AL). Gowdy was behind the plate. Muddy popped a high, lazy foul back of the plate. It looked like an easy out. Gowdy threw off his catcher's mask and went after the pop-up. But he threw his mask right in his own path. He stepped on the mask and his foot stuck. Gowdy tried to shake it off while keeping his eye on the ball. Hobbling in a panic, he stumbled as the ball plopped down beside him. Ruel was fired up by the second chance Gowdy had given him. He hit a double. The next batter followed with a hit that sent Ruel to home plate with the winning run—and the world championship.

Murderers Row

There have been many great Yankee teams, but the 1927 Yankees may have been the best team of all time. They earned the nickname "Murderers Row" because their powerful hitters destroyed opponents. The 1927 Yanks won 110 games, led by Babe Ruth and Lou Gehrig. Ruth hit 60 home runs that season. No other American League *team* hit more than 56! Gehrig was equally great. He hit 47 homers. He set a major league record of 175 runs batted in. Second baseman Tony Lazzeri and left fielder Bob Meusel each drove in more than 100 runs.

It was no surprise when the Yankees ended the season by sweeping the World Series. They beat the Pittsburgh Pirates (NL) in four games. But the *way* they won was surprising. Ruth hit two home runs in the four games, but no other Yankee hit even one. Gehrig had only four hits. Luckily, the Yankee pitchers came to the rescue. Led by future Hall of Famers Waite Hoyt and Herb Pennock, the Yankees allowed the Pirates to score just ten runs in the series.

Lou Gehrig coming home

Babe Ruth's "Called Shot"

A Babe Ruth special made the 1932 World Series famous. It happened in game three at Wrigley Field in Chicago. In the fifth inning, the Cubs and Yanks were tied 4-4. The Babe came to bat and the fans went wild. They were counting on him! Babe taunted the Cubs pitcher by holding two fingers high after each pitch. Two balls, two strikes. Two fingers held high. Was Babe's signal showing the count? Or was it to show where he intended to slam a home run? Everyone was sure Babe was calling the shots. Sure enough, on the next pitch, he hit a mighty blow. The ball sailed high and away, disappearing behind the scoreboard and bleachers. It went just where the Babe had seemed to be pointing! Babe circled the bases. For a moment the stunned crowd was silent. Then Yankee fans *and* Cub fans stood and cheered at the incredible feat.

People still wonder: Did Babe Ruth really call his shot? In 1932 there was no television. No one can look at the instant replay to decide. Even the players on the field disagree about what happened. Only Babe Ruth knew for sure. But the Babe never did set the record straight. He loved to tell people how he called his shot, but the story changed a little with each telling. Sometimes he hinted that he didn't call it. But the Babe had fun, and he gave the fans their money's worth. Whatever the truth, the Yankees went on to whitewash the Cubs. They won the series in four straight games.

For the Record

The 1932 World Series was the third Yankee sweep with Babe Ruth and Lou Gehrig in the lineup. Lou usually batted right after Babe. People were often so awed by a Babe Ruth special that they overlooked what Lou did. Lou had two home runs for the Yankees in that famous "called shot" game. In the 1932 series, Lou had three home runs to Ruth's two. He had nine hits to Ruth's five. He batted in eight runs to Ruth's six, and scored nine runs to Ruth's six. Lou batted .529 in the series. But anyone in the Babe's shadow usually ended up second banana!

Dizzy and Daffy

Dizzy Dean lived up to his nickname in the 1934 World Series. The brilliant right-hander pitched for the St. Louis Cardinals (NL). So did his younger brother, Paul Lee, or "Daffy." Dizzy won two games and lost one in the 1934 World Series. Daffy won the other two games. The brothers pitched a total of 44 innings. It was Dizzy's shutout against the Detroit Tigers (AL) that won the seventh and deciding game for the Cardinals. They defeated the Tigers, four games to three. Dizzy Dean was named the National League's Most Valuable Player (MVP) that year.

A Hit for Everyone

The Yankee hitters were awesome in the 1936 World Series. In game two the Yanks set a new series record by winning 18-4. Every player had at least one hit and scored at least one run. The team batted .302 for the series and outscored the Giants 43-23. The Yankees (AL) beat the Giants (NL), four games to two.

The $50,000 Snooze

Tiger shortstop Dick Bartell took a mental snooze at a crucial moment. It was in the seventh and deciding game in the 1940 World Series. The Detroit Tigers (AL) were winning 1-0 over the Cincinnati Reds in the bottom of the seventh. The Reds' Frank McCormick was on second base when the next batter, Jimmy Ripple, hit a double. McCormick thought the ball might be caught, but when it hit the wall he ran for third base. Bartell caught the throw from the right fielder. Instead of turning around, Bartell stood still, calmly turning the ball over in his hands. McCormick ran for home. The alarmed Tiger infield yelled to Bartell and waved their arms, but it didn't help. McCormick crossed home plate to tie the game. Seconds later Ripple scored the winning run. It seems Bartell thought that McCormick was home long before he got the ball. He was thinking only about holding Ripple on second base. Bartell's "snooze" cost the Detroit Tigers the world championship. And it cost them the $50,000 difference between the first-place and second-place winnings. Cincinnati was thrilled. It was their first World Series victory in 21 years!

Dick Bartell
takes a "snooze".

17

No Goats, No Wins, No Kidding

At the 1945 World Series, Chicago Cubs officials would not let fan Billy Sianis and his goat into Wrigley Field. Chicago (NL) lost the series to the Detroit Tigers (AL). The Cubs didn't finish in first place again until 1984. They invited Sianis's nephew and the goat's cousin to Opening Day at Wrigley.

Speedy Enos Saves the Series

For one of the best baserunning shows of all time, it's the 1946 World Series. The St. Louis Cardinals (NL) were playing the Boston Red Sox (AL). Enos Slaughter, Cardinal right fielder, was on first base. The score was tied with two outs late in the seventh game of the series. Cardinal Harry Walker then hit a line drive to center field. Slaughter was ready to run. He exploded off first. Boston shortstop Johnny Pesky took the throw from the outfield and whirled to throw the ball to third base. That's where he expected Slaughter to be. But instead of stopping at the base, Slaughter rounded third at full speed.

Enos Slaughter sliding home and winning the Series

He flew on toward home plate. By the time Pesky threw home, Slaughter was safe. He had scored successfully on a single to win the series for the Cardinals.

Memorable Moments in 1947

The New York Yankees (AL) beat the Brooklyn Dodgers (NL) four games to three in the 1947 series. The series had some memorable moments! In game four, Yankee Bill Bevens had a no-hitter going until the ninth inning. In a no-hitter, the pitcher does not allow a single hit to the rival team in the entire game. But batters can still get on base. The pitcher might walk some batters, or hit a few with pitched balls. Or the pitcher's teammates might make errors behind him, allowing a rival player to reach base or even score. The Dodgers had two outs and two men on base. Then Dodger Harry "Cookie" Lavagetto came up to bat. Lavagetto hit a double off the right field wall to ruin the no-hitter and give the Dodgers a 3-2 win.

Game six brought a famous World Series catch. Dodger outfielder Al Gionfriddo robbed Yankee Joe DiMaggio of a home run that would have tied the score. He caught DiMaggio's 415-foot drive with two Yankees on base. His catch saved the game for Brooklyn. They won, 8-6.

Yogi

Yogi Berra was a star Yankee catcher and outfielder during the 1940s, 1950s, and 1960s. He holds World Series records for games played (75), at bats (259), hits (71), and doubles (10). He appeared in 14 series and hit 12 home runs. This placed him just behind two other Yankee greats, Mickey Mantle and Babe Ruth.

The Brooklyn Dodgers and the New York Giants during the Pennant playoffs

The Homer Brooklyn Never Forgot

In 1951 two great rivals—the Brooklyn Dodgers and the New York Giants—ended the season tied for first place. League rules called for a three-game playoff series. The winner of two games would go to the series. Loyal Brooklyn fans, and almost everyone else, called the Dodgers the wonder team. They had stars like Jackie Robinson, Roy Campanella, Gil Hodges, Duke Snider, Pee Wee Reese, and Carl Furillo. How could the Dodgers fail to win the pennant?

Millions waited to see how the Giants-Dodgers rivalry would be settled. The score was tied 1-1 at the end of seven innings. Both teams had ace pitchers on the mound. But in the eighth, the Giants' Sal Maglie faltered. The Dodgers scored three times. It looked like it was over for the Giants. Then

Dodgers pitcher Don Newcombe faltered in the ninth. He gave up three hits and one run before being yanked. Young Ralph Branca took his place. The Giants' Bobby Thomson came up to bat with two men on base. On Branca's second pitch, Thomson connected. The ball sailed into the stands and the Giants scored three runs! By a score of 5-4, the Giants won the National League pennant. Gloom settled on Brooklyn. Four decades later, Brooklyn fans still mutter to themselves about that fateful hit off Bobby Thomson's bat. After the pennant playoffs, the New York Yankees (AL) defeated the Giants (NL) in the 1951 World Series, four games to two.

Bad Call

The New York Yankees played the Brooklyn Dodgers in the 1952 World Series. In the bottom of the tenth inning of the fifth game, the umpire blew a call at first base. With the score tied 5-5, Yankee pitcher Johnny Sain hit a slow roller to second baseman Jackie Robinson. Jackie threw late to first. But the umpire called Sain out before the throw even arrived! The player and coach argued loudly, but the umpire stuck by his call. It was such a bad call that even the commissioner of baseball refused to back him up. The happy Dodgers scored a run in the top of the eleventh inning to win the game 6-5. Photos showed that Sain's foot was firmly on the base bag while the ball was still several feet away from the first baseman's glove. The commissioner chose not to defend the umpire. Instead he said, "If I owned a newspaper, I'd blow that picture up to six columns." The *New York Times* did! One picture was worth a thousand words.

Five in a Row

In 1953 the Yankees (AL) won their fifth straight World Series. No team ever did that before, and none have done it since! Casey Stengel became the first manager to match five straight pennants with five straight world championships. And he did it in his first five years as manager of the Yankees!

Way to Go, Willie!

Willie Mays made a historic catch in the opening game of the 1954 World Series. The New York Giants (NL) played the Cleveland Indians (AL). The Indians were at bat. The score was tied at 2-2 in the seventh inning. Indians slugger Vic Wertz hit a mighty drive. It sailed to the deepest part of the oval-shaped Polo Grounds, the Giants' home field. At the crack of the bat, Giants center fielder Willie Mays turned and raced. He ran until his glove met the ball. He caught it with his back to the infield, some 460 feet from home plate! He whirled and threw

Willie Mays making a historic catch

the ball to the infield to keep the base runners from running. That ball would have been a homer in any other ballpark. It was the turning point for the Giants. The Indians never recovered and lost the series in four games straight. Mays's famous catch became part of baseball legend.

It Doesn't Get Any Better!

It was October 8, 1956. The New York Yankees were locked in a struggle with the Brooklyn Dodgers. The Dodgers had a fearsome lineup of great hitters. They had Roy Campanella, the famous catcher; Duke Snider, the famous slugger; Gil Hodges, Pee Wee Reese and Jackie Robinson. Any pitcher facing them would be worried! But not Don Larsen. His Yankee teammates nicknamed him Gooneybird, because he didn't take many things seriously—not even pitching. He baffled the Dodger greats, mowing them down inning after inning. Not one of the Dodgers' 27 batters reached first base on a hit, a walk or an error! By the end of the afternoon, the Yanks had held their 2-0 lead. And their pitcher, Don Larsen, had made history. He pitched a perfect game—a no-hitter in which no batter reaches base the entire game, either by hit, walk or error. It was the first and—to date— the *only* perfect game in World Series history.

White Sox, Black Sox, Go-Go Sox

In 1959 the Chicago White Sox (AL) took their first American League pennant since the Black Sox threw the 1919 World Series. They were known as the Go-Go Sox because of their hustle on the base paths. The Los Angeles Dodgers (NL) took the series, four games to two.

Three Game Heroes

The 1960 World Series had some highlights! The teams were the New York Yankees (AL) and Pittsburgh Pirates (NL). Whitey Ford started two games for the Yankees. He pitched shutouts in both. The Yankees won by scores of 10-0 and 12-0, thanks to Ford. In game seven, Ford was overshadowed. The Yankees led 7-4. Then the Pirates started scoring. The final three runs came on a home run hit by Pirates catcher Hal Smith. Suddenly, Smith was the man of the hour. Next, the Yankees tied the score in the top of the ninth. That paved the way for another game hero. Bill Mazeroski hit a homer over the left center field wall. Mazeroski's hit won the game...and most of the fame. The Pirates won four games to three.

A New Pitching Record

In the 1961 World Series, the New York Yankees (AL) met the Cincinnati Reds (NL). Yankee Whitey Ford completed 32 consecutive innings of scoreless pitching in World Series play. His feat erased the record held by Babe Ruth with 29 2/3 innings in 1918. The Reds dropped the series to the Yankees.

After the loss, the Reds rebuilt their team. The result was the Big Red Machine that dominated baseball in the 1970s.

Mickey

The New York Yankees were on top in the 1950s and 1960s. Their center fielder, Mickey Mantle, had a lot to do with the team's success. In turn, the team's success enabled Mickey to set many World Series records. He played in 65 series games, second only to Yogi Berra. He hit 18 home runs, a record. He scored the most runs, 43. He had the most runs batted in, 40. He had the most bases on balls, 43. And he had the most strikeouts, 54.

Changing of the Guard

The St. Louis Cardinals (NL) beat the New York Yankees (AL) in the seventh game to win the 1964 World Series. The game was the last post-season appearance for Whitey Ford and Mickey Mantle. And it was the second World Series loss in a row for the Yankees. Only in 1921 and 1922, in their first two series ever, had the Yankees lost twice in a row. In between, they won 20 of the 25 series they played in.

Boston's Impossible Dream

Boston thought it might never recover from the retirement of Ted Williams at the end of the 1960 season. Along came Carl Yastrzemski, the left fielder who replaced Williams. At first Boston fans howled at him because he wasn't Williams.

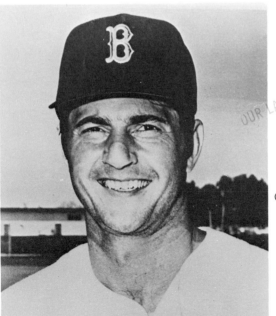

Carl Yastrzemski

But Yaz won over the fans in 1967 with one of the greatest years any player has ever had. In the final two games of the season, Yaz had seven hits in nine at bats as Boston beat Minnesota to clinch the American League pennant. Boston fans called it their Impossible Dream pennant.

Yaz led the Boston Red Sox (AL) to the 1967 World Series. They played the St. Louis Cardinals (NL). But led by Lou Brock's .414 batting average and his seven stolen bases, the Cardinals won. They beat the Red Sox four games to three, ending Boston's Impossible Dream.

Yer' Out!

It was the opening game of the 1968 World Series. The Detroit Tigers (AL) and the St. Louis Cardinals (NL) each had a powerhouse pitcher. For Detroit, it was Denny McLain. McLain was the first pitcher since 1931 to win more than 30 games in a season. For St. Louis, it was Bob Gibson. Gibson had 22 wins and an earned run average of 1.12. That means barely one run a game in over 34 games and 305 innings pitched. But it was no match. Gibson mowed down the Tigers. He set a series record with 17 strikeouts. The Cardinals won that opening game 4-0. But the 1968 World Series went to Detroit, four games to three.

The "Miracle Mets"

The New York Mets (NL) had been picked for last place in the 1969 season. The Mets hadn't been lucky since they were newly franchised in 1962. In their first season they were the laughingstock of baseball. Casey Stengel was the Mets' first manager. He had managed the Yankees to five champion-

26

1969 World Champion New York Mets

ships in a row (1949-1953). In his early days with the Mets, a frustrated Casey once asked: "Can't anybody here play this game?"

But in 1964 things began to change. A new stadium, Shea, was built in Queens, New York, and the Mets surpassed the Yankees as the area's favorite. The baseball farm system started sprouting good young players like Tom Seaver and Jerry Koosman. And in 1969, the Mets showed the world. It was the pitching of Seaver and Koosman that drove the Mets. A 100-1 shot in spring training, the Mets stayed close to the Chicago Cubs through the summer. They passed them in early September to win the division by eight games. Then they beat the Atlanta Braves in three straight playoff games to win their first pennant. After an opening-game loss in the World Series, the Mets won four straight from the Baltimore Orioles (AL). On October 16, 1969, the miracle year was complete. The New York Mets won the World Series, setting off a wild celebration in the streets of New York.

Lights! Camera! Action!

The 1971 World Series was the first to be played at night. It was won by the underdog Pittsburgh Pirates (NL). They beat the Baltimore Orioles four games to three. Roberto Clemente, the Pirates' right fielder, hit .414 and two home runs.

Three in a Row for the A's

The Athletics had a topsy-turvy history. They started in 1901 as the Philadelphia team in the new American League. Connie Mack managed the team for 50 years, winning five world championships. In 1955 the A's moved west to Kansas City. Charles O. Finley bought the team and shifted it to Oakland in 1968. It was a winning team, with players like Jim "Catfish" Hunter, Reggie Jackson, Sal Bando, Rollie Fingers, Gene Tenace, Bert Campaneris, Dick Green, and Vida Blue. The Oakland Athletics (AL) won three straight World Series. They won in 1972, 1973 and 1974. Only the A's and the Yankees of 1936-1939 and 1949-1953 had won three straight World Series titles.

Designated Runner Off Base

During the 1974 World Series, Herb Washington proved what fans and players already knew. The designated runner had no place in baseball. The idea was the brainchild of Oakland A's owner Charlie Finley. Finley had signed Washington, a track speedster, to play as a pinch runner. His job was to steal bases. He would never need to hold a bat or wear a glove. Washington had proudly donned his Oakland uniform for the 1974 season. But he had only 30 steals in 48 attempts.

Finley was under fire for his designated runner idea. But he was patient. He waited for the World Series to prove that his idea would work. He counted on Washington's speed and daring to win for the A's in a tight spot. Washington's golden chance came in the ninth inning of the second game. The Los Angeles Dodgers (NL) led, 3-2. Pinch runner Washington was poised to get the tying run. He edged away from first, itching to get to second. He stared at the pitcher. The pitcher stared back. Suddenly the pitcher made his move. Slap! The ball hit the glove of first baseman Steve Garvey and Washington was tagged out! The designated runner was out—and out of baseball the following year.

Herb Washington, a runner, not a ballplayer

The Series Baseball Won

The 1975 World Series could not have come at a better time. Baseball was losing fans to other sports. "Monday Night Football" drew many new viewers. Others were writing off baseball as a dull, old-fashioned game. But the 1975 series put baseball back in first place with most sports fans. It had late-inning tension, key hits and unforgettable plays. Carl Yastrzemski still says, "I've always thought baseball was the winner of that World Series." The Cincinnati Reds (NL) and Boston Red Sox (AL) were the teams that did it.

Cincinnati and Boston were the first professional baseball towns. It seemed fitting that they were the ones to bring a new surge back to baseball. The Cincinnati Big Red Machine was moving into high gear in 1975. The Reds had won 108 games during the year. Their lineup of Pete Rose, Joe Morgan, Johnny Bench, Tony Perez, Ken Griffey, George Foster, Cesar Geronimo and Dave Concepcion was one of the top groups of hitters ever on one team.

The Red Sox looked like baseball's new dynasty. They had the greatest rookie pair in big league history, Fred Lynn and Jim Rice. Together with Carl Yastrzemski, Carlton Fisk and Dwight Evans, they made opposing pitchers dread coming to Boston. The Red Sox had won 95 games. They swept the three-time world champion Oakland A's to win the League Championship Series.

Both cities were long overdue to win a World Series. Cincinnati had not won the title since 1940. The Red Sox hadn't won it since Babe Ruth pitched them to victory in 1918. It would all come down to the last inning of the seventh and final game!

The Best Game Ever Played

When the teams returned to Boston for game six, the Reds were ahead three games to two. But rain washed out play for three straight days. When game six finally started, it was worth the wait.

Game six of the 1975 World Series has been called the best championship game ever played. It kept millions of Americans up past midnight, waiting to see how it would end. Boston trailed 6-3 in the bottom of the eighth. They had two runners on base and two outs. Sox pinch hitter Bernie Carbo smacked a hit into the bleachers and game six took on a new identity. Strange, memorable things started to happen. The Red Sox nearly ended the game in the ninth inning. They

The 1975 World Series, the Boston Red Sox vs. the Cincinnati Reds

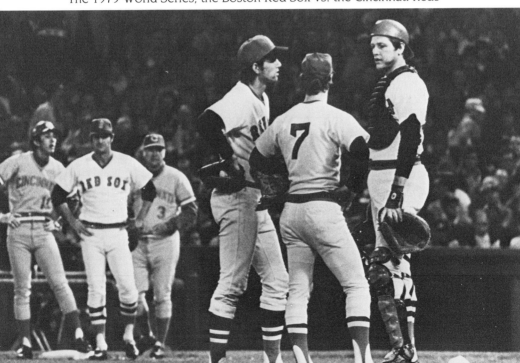

loaded the bases with no outs—then failed to score! In the eleventh, after midnight, the Reds looked like they were going to take the lead when Dwight Evans made a spectacular catch to complete a double play—two outs. On and on they played. It was past midnight when Carlton Fisk came up to bat. The score was still tied 6-6. Fisk smacked a hit that clanged off the left field foul pole, high over the wall of Fenway Park. Fisk whooped and galloped around the bases, jumping on home plate to end the game at 12:34 in the morning. The Red Sox won, 7-6. Carlton Fisk ran a victory lap around the outfield. Fenway fans stood and cheered. The Red Sox organist played the *Hallelujah Chorus*. Church bells rang and car horns blared in towns across New England.

The series was now tied at 3-3. The next day, October 22, the Cincinnati Reds won game seven and the 1975 World Series. But game six had taken its place as one of the best World Series games ever played.

Mr. October

Reggie Jackson was called Mr. October for a good reason. He thrived during the pressure of play-offs and World Series. He proved it again in the 1977 World Series. This was his first season as a New York Yankee. The Yankees (NL) faced the Los Angeles Dodgers (NL). Reggie blasted three home runs in the final game. The Yankees won the game and the series, beating the Dodgers. It was the Yankees' first World Series win in 15 years!

The 31-year-old Jackson became the first player to hit five homers in a series, including three in one game. The only

Reggie Jackson, reaching for the Series

other player ever to hit three in one game was Babe Ruth. The Babe did it twice. "The Babe was great," said Jackson. "I was only lucky."

Worth Celebrating!

It was the top of the ninth with two outs, bases loaded. The Philadelphia Phillies (NL) led the Kansas City Royals (AL) 4-1. It was the sixth game of the 1980 World Series. Police and trained attack dogs ringed Veterans Stadium. They were ready to control the celebration about to break out. Tug McGraw fired a fastball past Kansas City's Willie Wilson for strike three...and the Phillies won. Pitcher Steve Carlton, series MVP Mike Schmidt and Pete Rose had finally done it. They had just won the first championship in the Phillies' history.

Baseball Remembers Its Own

Former Philly Joe Oeschger threw out the first ball in the 1983 World Series in Philadelphia. For Joe, it was more than a welcome home to Philadelphia. The honor was baseball remembering one of its greats. It had been over 60 years since Joe Oeschger pitched the longest game in baseball history. The 26-inning marathon took place in 1920. Joe was pitching for the Boston Braves against the Brooklyn Dodgers. The game was called on account of darkness with the score tied at 1-1. Some sportswriters stated that Joe would never pitch again after that 26-inning game. But in 1921, Joe won 20 games for the Boston Braves. And 66 years after leaving the Philadelphia Phillies, he was given the honor of being asked to throw out the first ball in the World Series in Philadelphia. By the way: that 26-inning game used only three baseballs. Today's teams prepare five dozen balls for each game!

Joe Oeschger

Firsts in 1987

Before any games were completed, any runs scored or any heroes made, the 1987 World Series had set a mark. For the first time in its 84-year history, the World Series was being played indoors. The Hubert H. Humphrey Metrodome, home of the Minnesota Twins, was the site. Other records were set at the close. For the first time in series history, the championship team had failed to win a game on the road. And the first World Series had been won indoors.

Against All Odds: The Twins Magic

The "Twinkies" hadn't won a post-season game in 22 years. They had been a 150-1 long shot to win the 1987 World Series. Those were serious odds.

This series proved how inspiring a good home crowd can be. When the Twins returned from its unexpected American league play-off victory in Detroit on October 12, 55,000 raving fans met them at the Metrodome. In every game played during the World Series, the home team won. The series opened in Minnesota. The Twins jumped to a two-game lead. The next three games, played in St. Louis, were won by the St. Louis Cardinals (NL). Then the teams went back to Minneapolis and the Twins' dome. The Twins won games six and seven before deafening home crowds.

The fans were an important part of this series. Loyal hometown fans rocked the dome's roof with their cheers. Sellout crowds waved "Homer Hankies"—handkerchiefs imprinted with the Twins' logo. Twins fans never quit screaming for their team.

The players, the coaches, rookie manager Tom Kelly and the fans combined to give Minnesota a winner. Other teams have come from nowhere to win the World Series. Other cities have exploded with joy. But a team wins for the first time only once. The Minnesota Twins had the magic in 1987.

The Metrodome

Can't Hear You!

Dr. Bill Clark thought the noisy Metrodome helped the Twins win the series. He was the scientist—and Cardinals fan—who checked it out. Dr. Clark used a tiny meter to measure the noise level made by cheering fans in the Metrodome. Dr. Clark claimed the noise levels in the Metrodome were twice as loud as those in Busch Stadium, home of the Cardinals. He felt that because the Cardinals weren't used to the loud noise, they found it hard to play their best. The Cardinals made four errors in Minnesota during the series. The Twins made none. The Cardinals lost all four games in Minnesota. Many fans in Dr. Clark's section at the Metrodome wore earplugs. But they cheered as loudly as ever for their team.

When Once Was Enough

Oakland's Dennis Eckersley is one of baseball's all-time best relief pitchers. When he enters the game, usually in the ninth inning to finish off the game, he gets the job done. Dennis had 50 saves in 1988 including post-season. But he got a surprise in the ninth inning of the opening game of the 1988 World Series. In his only at bat, Los Angeles Dodger (NL) Kirk Gibson pinch-hit a home run off Eckersley's pitch. Gibson had not started the game. He could hardly walk due to sprains and strains. When he was called upon to pinch-hit, Gibson winced with pain at every swing. But with a man on base and the count three balls and two strikes, he connected. Gibson drove an electrifying hit into the right field seats.

Kirk Gibson drives an electrifying hit.

As Gibson limped around the bases, the fans in Dodger Stadium went wild. The A's were stunned. Fans wondered if Gibson would be able to make it to home plate. It was one of the most dramatic home runs in baseball history. Kirk Gibson became the seventh player to end a World Series game with a home run...and the only one to bring his team from behind while doing it. That at bat was to be Gibson's last appearance in the 1988 World Series. But he helped launch the underdog Dodgers to a World Series triumph in 1988. Read on for more.

A Date with Destiny

The Oakland Athletics (AL) had not had a winning season since 1981. In 1988 they steamrollered their way to the American League pennant. Their main basher was Jose Canseco, who had become the first major league player in history to hit 40 or more homers and steal 40 or more bases in a season. First baseman Mark McGwire had hammered out 32 homers and batted in 99 runs. Canseco and McGwire were called the Bash Brothers because they celebrated their home runs by bashing their forearms together. The A's had good reason to think they would beat their California cousins, the Los Angeles Dodgers, in the World Series.

The Los Angeles Dodgers surprised even themselves by winning the National League pennant. They did, however, have Orel Hershiser. He had ended a season by pitching six straight shutouts and a record-setting streak of 59 straight scoreless innings. They had Kirk Gibson and Mike Marshall to hit. And they must have had a date with destiny. They won games one and two. Hershiser pitched a shutout in game two

Jose Canseco at bat

and held the mighty A's scoreless. The Oakland steamroller was getting flattened by the lightweights from Los Angeles. In game three, Mark McGwire sent a hit over the fence to give Oakland a 2-1 win. The Dodgers were still one game up in the series. Then came game four.

The Dodgers' entire lineup for game four had hit fewer home runs than the A's Jose Canseco. But just before game four, the Dodgers got fired up. They heard a TV sportscaster say that without Kirk Gibson and Mike Marshall, who was forced out of game three with an injury, the Dodgers might have the weakest hitting team ever to play in a World Series. The Dodgers screamed, "We'll show him!" They won game four. Canseco, who hadn't had a hit since his grand slam in game one, said, "This is a shock. This is a tough thing to swallow." In game five, Hershiser pitched the Dodgers to another win for the world championship. He had allowed only

Orel Hirshiser pitches the Dodgers to another win.

two runs in his two World Series wins. The Dodgers' World Series victory had as much to do with players like Mike Davis and Mickey Hatcher as it did with Gibson and Hershiser. Davis was playing only because of Marshall's injury. He hit a big blast homer in game five. Hatcher had hit only 35 homers in 2,557 career at bats. He hit a two-run homer in game five. When Hershiser was named the MVP, he held up his trophy. He yelled to his underdog team, "Hey guys, this is for you!"

The Battle of the Bay Becomes the Rattle of the Bay

The 1989 World Series was played between the San Francisco Giants (NL) and their neighbors from across the San Francisco Bay, the Oakland Athletics (AL). The A's won the first two games. As the two teams were about to start game three, a powerful earthquake struck their cities. The series was delayed nine days while the Bay Area recovered. This became the longest series on record even though it ended in the minimum number of games. One player grew a beard between games 2 and 3.

As part two of the World Series began, the A's rocked the Giants twice to complete their sweep. Oakland outscored the Giants 32-14, tying the Yankees for the highest run differential ever in a four-game series. (The Yankees outscored the Chicago Cubs 37-19 in 1932.) Pitchers Dave Stewart and Mike Moore had two wins apiece. A record eight different players homered to help Oakland to a series-high .582 batting average. Rickey Henderson batted for the cycle and stole three bases. Dave Henderson became the new Mr. October with a .923 slugging percentage. Terry Steinbach drove in a team high—seven runs. Tony Phillips made three sensational plays at second in the final game. In 1989 the A's were an extraordinary team. And they played in the most extraordinary World Series in history.

Red-Hot Reds Shock A's with World Series Sweep

Baseball experts didn't give the Cincinnati Reds (NL) much respect during the 1990 baseball season. No one thought they had a chance against the awesome Oakland Athletics (AL) in the World Series. In 1990 the underdog Reds did what no one said they could do. They won the first four games for a World Series sweep! The Oakland Athletics became the first team to get swept in a World Series the year after sweeping one.

Reds pitcher Jose Rijo had once been on the Oakland team. In 1987, he was sent away from Oakland as a 22-year-old who would never grow up. In 1990, Rijo was chosen the World Series Most Valuable Player. He had allowed one run in 15 1/3 innings against his former team. He won both games he pitched in the sweep. Chris Sabo and Billy Hatcher of the Reds had nine hits apiece in the series that got Cincinnati some respect.

Jose Rijo

The Little League World Series

The Little League World Series started in 1947 when Williamsport, Pennsylvania, whipped Lock Haven, Pennsylvania 16-7. The series is still going strong. All 9,000 tickets are free, but 90,000 fans crowded around Lamade Stadium in Williamsport to watch the game. Little League World Series games are six innings long. The Little League World Series is the second longest running event on "ABC's Wide World of Sports." It marked 29 years in 1990. Only the Indianapolis 500 time trials beats that run.

Since 1967, teams from the United States have won only five Little League World Series titles. The most recent was in 1989, when Trumbull, Connecticut, defeated Kaohsiung, Taiwan, 5-2.

World Series Timelines

1903: The three bases Honus Wagner stole in the first World Series set a mark that has never been beaten.

1905: All five World Series games played ended as shutouts. The New York Giants defeated the Philadelphia Athletics four games to one.

1908: The Chicago Cubs became the first team to win back-to-back World Series Championships, winning in 1907 and 1908, and defeating Detroit both times.

1920: Elmer Smith of the Cleveland Indians hit the first grand slam home run in series history.

Elmer Smith hits the first
Grand slam home run.

1921: The World Series was broadcast on the radio for the first time. The New York Giants beat the New York Yankees, five games to three.

1928: Lou Gehrig of the New York Yankees set the record for home runs (four) and runs batted in (nine) in a four-game World Series sweep.

1948: Legendary 41-year-old pitcher Satchel Paige made his first and only World Series appearance with the Cleveland Indians.

Satchel Paige in his first and only World Series appearance

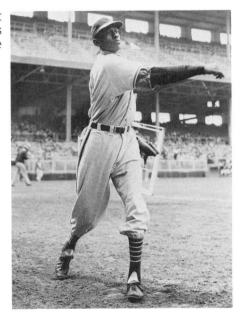

1979: Willie Stargell hit all three of the Pittsburgh Pirates' home runs during their seven-game triumph over the Baltimore Orioles.

1985: The Kansas City Royals became the first team in series history to rebound for a World Series victory after losing the first two games in its home park.

1986: The New York Mets became the second team in World Series history to rebound for a World Series victory after losing the first two games in its home park.

1987: This was the only World Series when the home team was the winner in all seven games.

1988: Don Baylor became the only player to play in three consecutive World Series for three different teams: the 1986 Boston Red Sox, 1987 Minnesota Twins and 1988 Oakland A's.

1989: Oakland became the first team to sweep the World Series since the Cincinnati Reds swept the New York Yankees in 1976.

1990: The Cincinnati Reds won their first division title since 1979. They became the first National League team to be in first place in the standings every day of a 162-game season. They won the World Series against Oakland.

Index